Why does it feel so late?

To Leonard.

I hope you enjoy
the book.

Nov 18/09.

Why does it feel so late?

Simon Thompson

VANCOUVER | NEW STAR BOOKS | 2009

NEW STAR BOOKS LTD.

107 — 3477 Commercial Street, Vancouver, BC V5N 4E8   CANADA
1574 Gulf Road, No. 1517, Point Roberts, WA 98281   USA
www.NewStarBooks.com   info@NewStarBooks.com

Publication of this work is made possible by the support of the Government of Canada through the Canada Council and the Department of Canadian Heritage Book Publishing Industry Development Fund, and the Province of British Columbia through the British Columbia Arts Council and the Book Publishing Tax Credit.

"The famous Cedar Apartments," "March ferry from Nanaimo," and "Renovation" are simultaneously appearing in *Local Knowledge* (Brooklyn, NY).

Cover by Mutasis.com
Printed on 100% post-consumer recycled paper
Printed and bound in Canada by Gauvin Press
First printing, November 2009

LIBRARY AND ARCHIVES CANADA CATALOGUING IN PUBLICATION

Thompson, Simon, 1967–
    Why does it feel so late? / Simon Thompson.

Poems.
ISBN 978-1-55420-046-7

    I. Title.
PS8639.H642W49 2009   C811'6   C2009–905063–3

Contents

Possession   1

I

How solitary lies the city   5
March ferry from Nanaimo   8
Heisenberg   11
The periodic table of elements holds us together   13
The river sounds deep and lies alone   14
How can you stand looking at the Skeena?   15
Marking papers   16
Frost's country   17
The famous Cedar Apartments   18
I gaffed a fish on Sunday   20
The only knowable thing   22
The Great Terrace Flood, 2007   23

II

Define "despair"   27
Springtime in Terrace   28
In the bonfire   30
Collage   31
Cement floor   32
Beetle black   33
Who calls?   35
Pancake breakfast   36
Renovation   37

III

Goldfish under ice 41

Northern haiku 2 51

Camping beside the homeless Québecois 52

The phone rings 53

Withdrawal 54

Darcy 56

Apples 59

I heard the flicker's grub-happy song 61

Why does it feel so late? 62

Possession

Sort the pop cans,
pick the lint from the dryer screen,
dust the mirror with a soft cloth.

A strange hand,
older and more frail than your own,
suddenly appears.

I

How solitary lies the city

In his last act,
he looks into the bottle of cooking wine,
hears a beautiful symphony and choir,
and sees right at the bottom among the dregs
the seven heavens of the Lord,
each one holding out the promise
of yet more happiness
than the one before.

The first heaven is of silver and in it are stars,
each with an angel, and strung out
like fish on plastic line.
It is found in the Chinese herb shop:
large glass jars
filled with dried deer penis and dusty bear paws.
In the back of the shop is an old Chinese man
with a ballpeen hammer and tin plate,
who beats out stars all day long under

the second heaven, which is of gold,
and is the domain of Jesus and John the Baptist,
who work on the Fraser
alongside the translucent bones of the giant sturgeon
and the waterlogged tree trunks
that float downstream to the booming yards.
The two men rest awhile
as the rising sun turns the water brilliant

and the steaming river begins to hide itself
from their holy sight and the bridge leading to

the third heaven of pearl,
and here Joseph parks
the number 22 bus he drives
from Knight Street to Clark Drive,
picking up the tired, the worried, and the drunk,
jerking them abruptly into their seats
as the electric motors quietly accelerate and
jostle the bus back into traffic.
His only pearls are the gifts of the compulsive masturbator
who stares from behind sunglasses
at the private schoolgirls in kilts
while the other riders shamefully ignore him,
full of hope the bus will soon come to the stop they all want,

the fourth heaven, which is of white gold
and holds the Angel of Tears.
He ceaselessly cries for the sins of the Filipina strippers
who wanted only a passport
but received instead a sacrament
of table dances, thong bikinis,
and a damp spartan apartment over a bar.
The Angel of Tears loves their brown skin and tiny bones,
drinks his pale blonde beer,
slips $5 in their G-strings
when they dance for him alone,
and in his reveries thinks of

the fifth heaven of emeralds
the colour of office tower windows,

reflecting the stalagmitic growth
of insurance buildings, forestry buildings, bank buildings.
The sun disappears from the green glass chasms
and electric heaters warm the sidewalk café dwellers
as they sip from tiny white cups of bitter espresso,
feel the strangeness of their own shaking hands
and watch the chaotic intersection of pedestrians
through the dusty windows of passing cars

far from the sixth heaven of rubies.
There sits sad, dignified Moses,
pulling at his beard and reciting
Thou shalt not kill!
over the blood-spattered corpse
buried deep in the park;
the fresh-turned soil hidden
by the new green of maple trees,
the stink disguised by the heavy salt breeze
corroding freighters at anchor in the harbour
as they wait to carry timber and sulfur

to the seventh heaven of diamonds and of God
and of the most exalted angels.
The heaven of heavens
is only the diaper- and pablum-scented air
inside the collapsing bright green house up
the treed avenue
where the young Vietnamese mother
comes with her baby to the window
at every stranger's passing
wearing a haggardly surprised expression
as if the thing she was least expecting had finally arrived.

March ferry from Nanaimo

The bulky dull ferry plows
through the flat water of the Strait of Georgia
like a bumblebee in winter.
The sun has set, and there is no light from the wheelhouse.
The captain is up there, though,
guiding his ship by the stars
and the lights of the tugboat to starboard,
three white lights,
clear and sloping like Orion's Belt.

No light from the wheelhouse,
for the captain, eyes closed,
is probing the night with his fingers,
going through the pockets of dark fabric
looking for something solid.
The soft clink of pennies and nickels
is replaced by the engine, clearly
banging away with a distant, vibrant tattoo.
The captain hears none of these things,
not even the bursts of static on the radio.
The captain sees nothing,
not even the green glow of the radar ghosts.

Somewhere his mind is watching the coloured planets,
the warning flashes of coastal lighthouses and buoys,
the growing dull fog of light
that envelops the emerging skyline.

The mate stands, transfixed, pale
as the atmosphere of the city ahead.
These are difficult waters,
narrow passages and pleasure craft:
a cigarette is waiting.
An accident is not out of the question,
and it's so dark,
the water so cold.
A man, swallowed up by the phosphorescent wake,
wouldn't last five minutes out there.
A man must keep watch.

"Mr. Smith," says the captain to the mate,
"I can hear your thoughts.
I can see through your eyes.
The ship is safe in my hands;
don't doubt it.
I can feel everything,
every bubble, every shift in the weather,
the breath of every person on this boat
as if it were my own.
Let me tell you that a woman is
drinking a cup of milk and
thinking of her childhood.
A man is smoking a cigarette
huddled against a wall beneath us,
buffeted by the wind.
Cigarette smoke is rushing along the turbulent air,
exhaled, lost.
He's thinking how hard it is to return to his wife
with his true love not far away.
Now a tiny flare of bright orange

tumbles from the smoker's fingers into the sea
and is doused.
The flag of the line is cracking insistently,
Mr. Smith,
and I see it and hear it all.
Take the wheel, Mr. Smith, and slow ahead."

The captain leaves the bridge,
and retreats to the steward's empty quarters.
As he unlocks the heavy door, he thinks,
I could slip overboard
like some secret sharer,
and fall as silently as ash
into the washing water about the ship.
I could get away.
But Vega, that northwestern pinprick
as bright as the moon,
a straight white comet tail through the waves,
that's the one that would show up my face.

Heisenberg

Skeena slides by wide
while sand bars shift
and with that shift goes the sense of land.

Skeena slides by plastic fluid
transparent one day
translucent the next.

Rain sweeps the hillsides
Spawners rattle the cobbles
water milky now with semen
now with silt.

The eye sweeps along the surface
finds a place   bubble
drifts in the current undisciplined
searches for the spot just lost.

The eye slips along the top
against the run of the surface reflects uneven light/sky
not polarized bottom invisible now
undulates green glass transformer.

Up the bank that burst last spring
so the water could follow itself and carve a passage
that is never fixed.

The eye staggers along the bank massive birch forced down
trunk shattered bark clapping metronomic with the speed of water
flat water drags behind a pool churning out in front
sudden surge the colour of eucalyptus
and the bottom is gone.

The periodic table of elements holds us together

Two-stroke oil slick and saltwater,
creaking dock boats
scuff with the tide and bump hollow:
waterline, red, fibreglass hull, white.

Against the wind and tide
resistance is only an imperfect vacuum.
Wood splits with the clime;
there's no stopping a bolt of cedar splitting
along the grain.

It's a part of a larger scheme:
the periodic table holds us together.

The river sounds deep and lies alone

The Skeena is a strong god
sometimes green and smooth
sometimes brown and rough

It moves mountains to the ocean
quickly and slowly
pauses for a while at bends then starts again

Just because I have fallen in the river doesn't mean I am the river
not baptized or transformed but carried only like a log
floating across one frontier and another

One must have a mind of summer
to see the god full of grit and sticks and power
to hear its scratching thumping voice
everything in itself excluding nothing
but the listener.

How can you stand looking at the Skeena?

How can you stand looking into the glacial haze of the Skeena?
How can you stand to cross the bolted timbers of the old bridge?

Many suspect I grieve a secret
long since washed downstream.

A raven's wings in flight form a certain angle
and some read this as a sign of impending doom,
but the grey tissue of smoke hanging about the smouldering
     campfires
the cottonwood pollen falling aimlessly into the water
is not a map or even a hint.

Marking papers

Might as well wave a pencil
at the Skeena as it mysteriously
slides away.

Might as well write my name
in the air with a blade of grass.

Frost's country

I think first of Frost
when I hear the buzz saw
rattling and snarling unseen
in the neighbour's yard
I wonder who holds the saw?
Are they prepared to meet the blade?

A saw is not benign at once ready to leap
tear the hand that feeds it:
stiff leather of the glove
pinky stuff of skin,
muscles and the bones that hold it all together
all tear under the whirling steel,
the nightmare smell of blood
all confused with the spice of cedar.

The neighbours toil away out of sight to build their shed,
the saw skirls to match their work.
Out behind the new-made walls
the neighbours cut away what's left of the day,
feel the torque of the saw as it cuts the load
always hungry for more.

The famous Cedar Apartments

The rain has stopped
for now.

Pale kids emerge
from the Cedar Apartments
to play on the lumpy infield at the junior high;
their evening late fall shadows are stretched tall
to reach me.

I watch my daughter
as she makes laps of the track,
her newly made bicycle circles encapsulate me;
I walk behind
in circles of my own.

Old patterns and lines intersect
every time I take a walk,
the slump-shouldered crane-necked figure that is me.
Buzzard-like,
I appear in old and damaged clothes
to be old and damaged.

Someone spent a lot of money on the school,
an architectural wonder of sheet metal
reflecting the shapes of a far-off range.

The word "fuck"
is painted in red letters on the library window,

the shadow of the word
falls on spinners full of paperbacks.

The apartment kids have no ball/no bikes:
they mill around,
mindlessly kicking the turf
with the toes of their basketball shoes.

One looks back to home;
television light emerges from sliding doors
over unused verandas piled high with junk.

The police go there every day,
pull people apart
to stop the yelling.

Our sun is swiftly eaten by a pregnant cloud,
flashes again and drops behind a western peak
on its way deep into the mountains.

I gaffed a fish on Sunday

I was not fishing but watching
when the fish took the bait
just below the surface of the Kalum
July colour chalkboard green.

The angler set the hook horsed the line in played the fish
surface film punctured by the muscular pulse of a tail
by a head set
to throw the hook.

The angler wound the tired spring in
and called up from the bank:
"Will you gaff him?"
I said I would.

"In the head.
Gaff him in the head."

I did what I was told
I got the fish through the eye
and blood poured from his head
like toxic smoke from a burning warehouse
the river thickened from the billowing clouds of red.
Belly up he hung at the bank
heaving and leaching and dying.

As the fisherman skittered down the rocks to grab his prize the jack
    convulsed
off the bank back into the current.

Both of us splashed in watered blood
head to foot.

I looked at the wet mark on the cobble
where the jack had been and bled
and words escaped me.

The only knowable thing

The live body of a sockeye
beats the wet rocks
a wet thud like an axe into a log.

I beat the blue and silver head
with a rock bloody gills the incomplete circle
of the swinging arm.
The mouth opens and closes drowning in the too thin atmosphere.

I cut open the cold white belly
unseam the layers of skin and fat
flesh curving in a cave of bones
undone as easily as a zip-loc bag
before the honed blade of my knife.
I see the viscera lying in one neat package
contemplate the pink labyrinth
and the discriminate mass of the purple liver.

I drop the guts in the river.

I'm sweaty with killing the river folds over and swallows the guts
I give away the meat as fast as I can.

The Great Terrace Flood, 2007

The river bank is crumbling to meet us
a dark mess of wet logs and roots.
Abandoned houses are married
with a ring of sandbags.

The river pulses up and down,
helicopters clatter overhead.

Watchers stand on the old bridge
as whole trees fall in
and float away rootballs up,
leaders nosing the river bottom
like curious pigs.

II

Define "despair"

To watch your father come drunkenly down the stairs
with purple lips crying that he's failed us all.
To lie in bed still drunk the morning after New Year's
listening to your daughter
pad down the hallway while you try to piece together exactly what
  it was
that you did: the shame of it all,
then being thrown out by an angry doorman.
You remember walking home in a T-shirt, snow falling hard, that
  long drunken
uphill walk home to the bed where your innocent wife soberly slept.

Springtime in Terrace

My daughter pokes the rotten crow
that died in last November's big windstorm,
knocked out power with its beak
and lay frozen in the ditch all winter.
She makes a noise like a crow as her stick traces the limp form,
probes its wet sleek feathers.

This is spring now or maybe just the end of winter
and spruce buds form
against the grey sky
forget that you saw
the brown sparrow that scrambled by,
the one with the blade of straw.

At this time of year,
tired, cranky winter
reduced in stature to threadbare patches of snow,
waits in the mountains hard with frost,
eager to swoop down and pluck out the darling buds of March
that idiot spring, babbling down the valleys,
trades for snow it collects from my backyard.
There the strawberry bed strangles itself with tendrils,
new but cold as earth.
What do these vibrant green fuses know?
They are dumb to the steadily working magic of spring
who releases unearthly vigour from the wet black mulch
of last autumn's leaves.

Come kind spring, eternally mild, eternally forgetful,
come from the centre of your silver cloud
while the music of frozen birds wakes around
and the earth is veiled in a shower of crocus and snowdrop.

In the bonfire

Boxes, branches, and newspapers
are transformed into enormous black cinders
that flutter away on the updraft,
a winter's worth of garbage into the sky:

Some handsome native kids
also float by,
heads shaved like monks,
boyishly-muscled and faces creased
in genuinely easy smiles.
I want to tell them
not to forget what they're doing.

Collage

A bunch of long and pale lilac sprays
in a jug
in the kitchen window
above the sink;
your face appears
composed of tiny mauve flowers.

Cement floor

The black beetle crosses the floor and goes
where no one goes.

I see it in the bathroom mirror
moving to a crack in the wall.

There are other worlds in sight;
ignore the wind
that turns the weathervane,
fuels the fire,
burns the forest,
drives the beetle into my house to walk across my floor:
a world so strange
where the salmon have vanished
just gone from the river,
the last orange from the bowl on the kitchen table.

What happened?

Reach out for the orange
or the bottom step on a darkened staircase
and that last step isn't there or is it?

Beetle black

Iridescent in the dampened world of concrete;
chemical smell
human effluvia
not a dream;
smell of humans rolling across the landscape
opposable digits plucking apples from the trees,
never mind sour apples rotten apples ripe apples all the same.
An August afternoon here
with voices going everywhere;
nowhere
is here
but I am here.

As are the roofers who spill nails from my roof:
smoke, laugh, wheeze,
whose voices reverberate unclearly
through the timber of the house.

What are they saying?
Elevated closer to what than I?

A transparent apple straight from the tree;
a fat blade of asparagus broken from the bed;
a tomato warm from the greenhouse,
or a joke with a flawless delivery.

What is there before or after the present
but silence and blankness,

forgetting how hard some work
and how some lie in the grass reading novels.

Who calls?

Throughout the house
a voice of wet newspaper,
rain plinking;
the newly blackened asphalt stinks,
colour television glows through plate glass.
Where did all the energy go?

Pancake breakfast

This morning I ate pancakes
outside a grocery store.
The cook passed me a paper plate,
and said, "Thanks for helping the sick kids."
A local celebrity smiled at me,
and on her ankle
I saw a blue tattoo of a dolphin
jumping over a crescent moon
into the Milky Way.

I thought to myself
she must be in a kind of hell
I don't yet recognize.

Renovation

The plastic airplane climbs and climbs;
the roofers lay shingle after shingle and descend
at the end of the hour
soaked in sweat, dousing themselves
with the cold spring water that comes by magic
from the hose.
The apples fall from the trees,
the peppers grow red in the green house and my daughter
grows taller and begins to look like her own person,
mournful and sad as an adult beaten
or as a child who knows that life
is not the open road
from which one descends like a pilot
fresh from the transatlantic.
Rather, she knows that one descends like a roofer
at the end of the hour, sweaty and slightly dopey
from the heat, wanting a cigarette and a dousing with cold water
drawn amazingly from some dark hole
beneath the surface or from some other place
but at that point not caring
from whence the water sprang,
and she kicks her ball across the lawn as the sun sets
and the ball rises and falls like a rainbow
according to a predetermined course that is beyond her
now or I hope is beyond her
that states when a thing shall rise and when a thing shall fall.

III

Goldfish under ice

Cloudy ice
filled with bubbles
and layers of matter:
willow leaves from the fall,
spruce needles,
dust and tiny brown fronds of cedar.

The goldfish never move
under the ice:
some are locked in;
some are upright,
bolt stiff but alive.
Here today,
here yesterday.

Hanging as if frozen,
the ice already inches thick
and the goldfish
still as a sunset in memory
or as photos of blimps
in an aerodrome.
Golden still under the ice;
an invisible black bottom.
I move my foot over them
and think about falling into water.
And in the black water
their frozen slow brains sense something
and move their fins,

still languid, not stiff at all,
guide them down to the bottom
away from the shadow of the foot,
away from a sun that had warmed
the water in which they basked beneath the ice.

But twenty below for a week,
the fish have become amber in ice:
their eyes have turned white blue,
their scales are perfectly fresh.

Did they again drift near the top to catch the rays of the sun
so far away?
Then grow sleepy with the rise of the mid-afternoon moon,
dozing off to be stuck to the top of their world
dreaming of springtime
and stuck fast like a penny in resin
in the bar in the Rainbow on Hastings.

The last place I ever ate a pickled egg,
bartender reached in with bare hand,
slapped it down at my place
white as fat:
glass of beer $1
pickled sausage
fights breaking out every few minutes.
No one did anything to stop the punchers;
they just got tired and sat down,
bleeding and winded.

I wander the edge of the pond,
step out on the ice.

I never learned to skate;
always came home bruised,
could never stop

Now the ice is three feet thick,
extends to the bottom.
I imagine
no place to hide now,
the ice crystals in their blood
dozy and aching;
the fingers of ice reaching down
to the black bottom.

I watched Mars float by:
the sky was clear
The wind flicked the lights
and Mars went by all rosy in heaven,
warm in the frozen black of whatever is out there;
I felt stuck to the top of my very own pond
though bundled in down and leather and wool.

I wondered why I have spent the last eighteen months
consumed and consuming,
wasting,
crippled.

Every day
checking the phone,
reading the mail,
parsing the faces
for the message that ends:

"we wish you luck
in other endeavours."

I will lie
I will fight
I will deserve
my endeavour.

Where is Vancouver?
It is not here.

The wind roars through the spruce trees
surrounding my house.

Am I awake or am I asleep?

Intermittently
I hear the wind
speaking in rushing tones.
Damn you! it says
and slams the gate,
throws around the plastic sled out front,
parts the grasses
and blasts grains of snow against my bedroom window.

I dream myself saying "Nothing is so boring as the dreams of
    others."

Wind pushes itself into every conversation;
it strips away all the warmth in the world.
It tires me out when I fight against it.

I don't want the wind
to come to my party;
I love the wind
but it must stay outside.

Crows as garbage bags
wind ripped and fluttering on the power line.
In this north wind that does not stop,
blows the snow sideways,
not snowing but snow blowing around:
snow devils.

How do we stop the sentence?

Driving along McConnell
with pulses of wind
traced by millions and millions of dry flakes
leaching from one bank of pines
to the opposite bank of pines,
swirling lit by headlights,
vision circumscribed by light
bouncing off snowflakes:
pulse,
light lost:
Now flying,
still the forest
black as a pupil.

And the subject of the poem
is I

Out of the sky
like Brueghel's Icarus,
my thin white legs disappear
just as naturally
into my own black pool.

float/don't float

With the blue white eyes of the fetus:
the eye is fooled again
in spring time;
the inanimate goldfish will float,
the crows will devour them choking them down whole.

When I was six
I went to hospital;
I remember the ward,
the bathroom a long way off,
the bed too high
and cold.

Because my feet were warped
and chafed inside of shoes;

My mother's feet:
bulges and knobs and crooks of their own.

and my occasional father
when he came to take me home;
his features in a certain light:
at dusk,
eyes in shadow,

bushy eyebrows,
evening sun glinting off the fearsome dome of his scalp.
thin lips murderously drawn with the state of traffic.
I was too scared to speak.

It's not the end of my world
because I once thought
my father was trying to kill me,
my mother was trying to kill my father
with butter and cake.

The world is cold for weeks on end;
the pond freezes to the bottom.

Sunny
day
thin section
clustered together like pennies.

Someday soon the air will be warmer;
the day after will be warmer still.
Ice will melt,
goldfish will float to the top
as human bodies float
down the Ganges,
wreathed in smoke and then
sinking slowly after.

Or the crows,
gingerly plucking the golden bodies
from the water.
They do not preen,

their reflection has no intent;
black eyes.

One summer,
I tried to take a picture
of a crow
but the film could not capture
the luminous black
of its feathers
or the glistening obsidian bead of its eye.

Rather what I got back was a picture of a black shape
to be filled in later.
This is the shape of possibility,
nervous with self-preservation,
looking left and right
before tearing at the food
swallowing something slimy and golden,
an act attracting other crows,
in turn pushing forward with black beaks
battering with black wings.

Every thing is hungry.
Every thing sticks in memory.

I walked through an overgrown lot,
saw an indigent sitting on his heels,
staring at the ground
a few feet from him.

As I got closer,
I saw he was watching intently

two other middle-aged indigents fucking ironically
missionary-style
in a depression in the ground.

The lot was not
empty.
The air was warm but the sky was grey:
summer in Terrace.

There was broken concrete,
the feet of a long-ago house,
glass among the dried grass
and a broken hydro meter sticking up
as if to say:
"I can still do it
if anyone ever comes back to live here
amongst this clump of bristling stuff;
there is still a shape to be filled in."

The man stood up
when he noticed me
and said, "You don't want to look at that,"
so I looked

and she looked right at me
and the guy on top of her
fully dressed
kept fucking her
lost or oblivious or determined.
She smiled blearily
as I passed.

When I turned back to look
she was pulling up her jeans,
the two men dusting her off
and I saw them,
all three totter away
happy and natural
as frozen goldfish in their infinite home.

Northern haiku 2

Nisga'a wolf jacket,
why do you piss on my lawn?
Shame your mother's crest.

Camping beside the homeless Québecois

Pot smoking,
beer drinking,
guitar playing,
bad teeth, the teeth of the poor.

Pork chops and carrots and potatoes for dinner,
cooked over the fire
in a frying pan.

They look like lifers from Kingston
and the woman has a broken nose,
goes to bed and starts to vomit;
the rest of them don't blink.

A bear runs across the road,
as skinny and leggy as a child;
the way it looked back at us:
disdain or wonder.

A trucker yelled at me today:
"Have some respect, you asshole!"

The phone rings

The dream of smoke that is ruptured
when the phone rings so late in the night,
I speak softly as if to honour the softness of evening
or the respectful tenderness of dark.
Who am I in my barely-lit kitchen
speaking in these intimate tones
to some one who could be a lover,
but instead is the seller
of a freezer load of meat.

Withdrawal

I went for a walk through the indelible spruce forest
again this morning
singing:
"Only today and just for this minute ..."
through the glory of the blow-down,
a round patch of trees perfectly toppled
inscribed on the hillside,
found the aspens growing in a line of green
brighter and newer;
I followed the green up the grade
to a clearing.

There, a mess of old concrete
slabs half submerged in rotted snow,
greening with algae, water fractured.
These were footings for a mill,
scraps of metal beams,
barrels and rope rusted to an auburn thread,
bolts set upright for absent plates dismantled or cut away
in a flash of acetylene flame.

Bottomless earth, broken rock, rainbow tongues of oil.
In every breath
the evil hopeful scent of decomposing wood and fungus.

High and cold,
I never saw the sun look so dull, so like a white letter on a white
    board.

After some time the forest will remedy itself
Of this unnatural broken plain
of still-sharp lines of work,
approach on leaf litter
borne as seed or spore
on long strings of rain.

By then I will be dead,
the wristwatch removed from my wrist
the complaining ceased;
others will mindlessly
kick remnants of iron
from the moss-covered ground.

Darcy

I went to Fort St. James this summer
to help bury an old friend.
He died of stomach cancer
a couple of days after marrying.
It was warm that burial day
and I sweated heavily in my black worsted suit.
The cottonwood leaves fluttered in the lake breeze,
and some people wept at the awful unfairness of it:
parents must predecease their children,
funerals should not happen on sunny days.
His bride smiled and seemed stunned
that so many would come to see her loved one off.

That night
four or five of us went to a bar and got dead drunk
and laughed a lot about dead Darcy.
How he dropped the transmission
out of his dad's truck
and tried to fix it with a stick.
It's just a way of coping,
to laugh at the dead.

I lost a story I wrote about Darcy,
and I regret the losing part,
but I remember the central image
of his silhouette, outlined in flames,
in front of the door of a beehive burner.
He would come over to my place

after work
to drink
at 2 in the morning.
I would go back to bed
and he would sit there on the Ikea sofa,
drinking his cans of Kokanee in the dark.
The buzzing of the mill's machines
ringing in his ears keeping him awake, alert.
He would always be gone in the morning.

Darcy liked drinking:
one night we lay in the bed of his truck,
drunk on my dad's wine,
watching a meteor shower.
It was another brilliantly clear, warm night,
the meteors falling like cosmic dandruff
as we lay on the cold steel of the truck bed
and forgot all of our 17-year-old troubles
in our drunken incomprehension of sky.

He always used to complain of stomach aches;
it must have started way back then.
He knew drinking only made it worse
and used to chew on antacid tablets
and drink Pepto-Bismol from the bottle,
just so he could keep drinking.
There wasn't a whole lot else to do
in Fort St. James;
drink and fuck,
and if you weren't fucking,
you had to be drinking.
Darcy definitely wasn't fucking anyone;

ever seen a skinny, stooped 17-year-old
with peach fuzz and acne?
That's how he will remain in my memory.

Outside the bar,
we drifted through the parking lot
and waved goodbye to the bride as she
disappeared in a friend's packed old station wagon,
her face distorted by the failed promise
of the evening,
by the condensation on the windows.
The night was warm
and it seemed perverse that Darcy
was not there
at all.

The bride went back to Prince George,
lives under the Darcy's last name.
That's all I know of it.

Apples

A twenty-foot ladder
emerges from the tree top
pointing brightly skyward.
There are hundreds,
maybe thousands of apples I have not picked,
will not pick.
I am tired of apple picking now.

All summer I watered the trees;
icy water from the town's spring flowed over the sun-dried earth,
trickled down among the roots
to produce these transparent apples
no one eats anymore.

My neighbour was made to eat them
when he was a boy;
apple sauce winter through,
a cellar full of jars.

The boughs bend near breaking
but do not break
with this unwanted crop of light green apples.

My wife wants to tear them out and start again
with saplings of crisp Fuji or tart Macintosh.
She sees barrels full,
and me upon the ladder with a satchel
like some poetic old man.

At night the only sound
is the earthy thud
of apples falling.

I heard the flicker's grub-happy song

The other day in dripping tones of fall
I heard summer's dry hiss weakly fail.

My wife wanders among the garden beds and fruit trees
cutting back dying foliage as it drains itself of green.

She has her hair wrapped in a scarf of pink gingham
and looks the image of a reaping peasant,
her pruning saw atonally stuttering,
bare and fruitless apple branches falling to the lawn.

Maple leaves glow and twist like a harvest flag
as kids on skateboards pass without comment,
their long glances and inscrutable faces of cloud blossom
rolling slowly past the figure now stooped among the iris stems.

Love's scrawl is clear without reference;
the garden is a clean piece of paper
where she yearly records its progress.

Why does it feel so late?

7:30ish February I find myself drifting out the door with wallet and
    keys in hand.
Evening air not cold enough for fall's rotting leaves to hide out;
I slink in between the creakings of my house
to conceal my mission from the ones whom I love or have promised
    to love.
I am waiting for someone to ask me quite simply to put things in
    order
from one through to ten
the ones and the things I think I love best
as I pause to consider the state.
This is still winter?
Snow slips away, grass is sodden, leaf buds are forming, dog shit is
    melting.
I've lately heard some experts say "Febuary" is OK
but I want "February";
it's the rue.

Fog pours over the mountain's lip;
the moon is magnesium bright
as the powerful lights of the liquor store gleaming two blocks away.
Moth/hence and through the electric double doors flinging
    themselves open
in obsequious welcome, the piles of booze, boxes and cases,
sweet alcoholic stink of empties.
I'm always the customer wandering back and forth, my foolish
    dance of indecision

lost in a snowstorm, making a choice between dying in this drift or
  that drift;
bored clerks in striped shirts;
wire racks as in a dime store bearing tons without buckling,
tiled floor so modern and easy to clean,
a dull pastel shine
and unobtrusive easy-listening music to calm the patrons.
There is something familiar about the way
in summer the wasps are drawn away from the windfalls that litter
  the lawn
to glass bells full of sugar water. They drown by the hundreds.
Can't the new recruits hear the muted desperate buzzing of their
  bottled-up familiars?

The closed circuit TV captures my pacing of shall I? Shall I?
. I am not interested in the endless selection;
I want the cheap, the hard, and the obvious,
The log trapped on the bottom of the river
hunting in the current, massive and awkward, swinging back and
  forth,
endlessly fidgeting like the ones who run so endlessly at the gym,
not blatantly worried, sweating and watching TV;
from experience, I know they will run
into themselves a few years later,
not fresh anymore but somewhere between frozen and thawed,
idly waiting for the light to change.

In the midst of a late winter snowstorm
the citizens of Terrace find that February has done its work;
the arctic outflows have dried out the known universe and frozen
  my pond to the bottom.

The cold dry air has poured through my house and chapped my
    skin,
leaving me as insubstantial as the moment
I emerged from the womb skinny as paper with beautiful hands
    and a body all blue;
a Bayeux knight in my parents' bed
my mother thought I would play the piano.
When I did not breathe for a while that plan disappeared
and for years I fluttered along until last Sunday;
I learned how to shape steel into weapon.

Stone after stone submerged in water, ground into slurry,
the edge of the chisel finer and finer
sharpened enough to cut out my iris. In this game that I play,
my chisel can slip and dive for my hand like a ravenous dog.
Around and around my hands guide the blade,
swinging in circles as if undecided about whom I must judge.
The top of the stone breaking and polishing when I'm not thinking,
only conducting the wave that flows through the sparrow,
eating its fill of the pile of seeds that spilled from the feeder with
    the help of the crows.
I've read that a chisel when blunt is more deadly.
A sharp chisel starts blood as if it will never stop;
infection comes as always, metal into me, the denial of this as
    pointless as hoarding books
for protection against the magic of traffic.
There is no mantra for objects.
For example, last Friday, the stove stopped working.
Exploded, in fact: a flash the colour of sulphur, the stench of metal
    burning not welding,
a little cloud of grey smoke moving silently toward the window.
The elements cooled: little, less, nothing more.

The repair man said if we put $200 in it, we'd have a 25 year old
    stove worth nothing.

And the next day, Saturday,
The television stopped working.
After a week
I began to miss the television,
all 20 inches of its low fidelity
one channel, one-pronged antenna coloured comfort.
I bought our TV, so seemingly modern back then,
from a pawnshop on Granville,
hauled it back on the bus in the rain.
That seemed like an accomplishment, a story.

But now I seem not to care about the television,
about images dancing, what's going on somewhere else.
I only watched hockey anyway, the news, to delay my bedtime.

Instead, I turn to the mirror;
I have shaved my face in the glass and I look younger than usual,
not puffy but lean, proud of myself.
7 PM; watching the clock that hangs in the kitchen,
blue and sea green, Prince Rupert's colours on a good winter's day.
It's soothing to stare
stare at the clock as it cranks out the seconds. My hand runs
    blindly,
searching for whiskers, the ones that I missed, but nothing is amiss.
7:01 PM and I am not drunk.
I shouldn't be noting this.
Why, I want to ask my wife, why does it feel so late?